Reflections on a Smile

Also by Lester Sawicki, DDS

Yin Ain't Yang
The Teeth Whitening Cure
Teeth In Mortal Combat
The Tao of Tooth

Reflections on a Smile

LESTER SAWICKI

© Copyright 2012 by Lester J. Sawicki, D.D.S.
5501A Balcones Dr #155, Austin, TX 78731

www.Tooth-Fight.com
www.Revolutiontooth.com
info@revolutiontooth.com

Library of Congress Control Number: 2012909292
ISBN: 9780984370641

Interior Design by William Groetzinger

Beauty, Love, Spirit

Charlene, Linda, Muchen

✷

All Earthly Joy Will Ultimately
Be Reflected In A Smile.

✤

Lips are seldom self-satisfied
with the smile they create.

✤ ✤

Frosty lips whose
upper lip walked and lower lip crawled
through rustling words of a
winter's tale ice stung with pains.

✤ ✤ ✤

In your lifetime being star struck
with a smile of love will be as close to the divine
your lips will ever experience.

✤ ✤ ✤ ✤

Touch my lips
to become intimate with the
smile hidden within.

Reflections on a Smile

Old lips crashed and surged
by a filthy trumpeting great wave
of voice without a smile.

Haunted lips took sanctuary behind a holy smile.

Squealing lips pursed straight up,
harnessed by foolish imaginings
swept blindly behind a flippant smile.

A Smile Is Like An Inner Thermostat.
You Can Turn It Up Or Down
And It Always Works To Benefit You.

The predatory smile leapt blindly from scarlet lips
like a slitting knife in final desperation.

Quivering lips lingered
smiling over juicy morsels
before scurrying the bits onto a
sprung up wildly lashing tongue.

The thrill of a vanishing smile is that
the lips can't sense how they might surprise you
and how they might not.

Your whispered smile is the only element
that can set my lips free.

A big sparkling aesthetic smile takes more credit
in today's world than wise words from erudite lips.

There's a great deal of uncertainty
in a smile that lips can't shake free.

Crooked smiling teeth, settled and bolted down
behind suddenly shuddered lips,
lurched into grinding instinctively
like gritty rusty bars of a bruxing rattling cage.

The Only Difference
Between A Smile And A Frown
Is In The Way Your Heart Speaks.

Reflections on a Smile

※

Lips singing a smile so sweetly
that birds gathered to listen.

※ ※

Lips so hard and plum dark blue
they might be a sea bottom beast sucking to tear
the heart out of your half wasted smile.

※ ※ ※

An obligatory smile is a division,
a way of not facing what the lips really mean to say.

※ ※ ※ ※

Lips have a job to instill blind erotic desire in a smile.

※ ※ ※

Vampire-fanged smile swiftly relished
the milky pink bolus slopping down the passageway
beyond the shadow moon lips.

※ ※

Experience isn't necessary for lips
to properly punctuate a perfect smile.

※

Lips awash with browning swallow mud
under a melting smile weary with wetting tears.

✻

A Smile Is Like Music On Your Face.

✻

The old howling beast's bitter smile
had curling lips ready to fling themselves like
birds sparking with wings of fire.

✻ ✻

The gift of lips is to conjure a feeling smile
with magical spontaneity.

✻ ✻ ✻

Perfect lips shape a smile's zenith once lost.

✻ ✻ ✻ ✻

Dried blood lips flame-flecked with rose hips
cursed threats hard and long
never known by a mumbly-dumbly smile.

✻ ✻ ✻

A joyous smile lost much of its strangeness to
lips once fearful and stuttered with a dark
shadow of silence by a single pointed finger
setting in crosswise salute.

Reflections on a Smile

Lips feel they are part of the body
but a smile is part of a larger entity beyond the senses,
even beyond life and death.

Cosmic lips shaped by a backward dimension
vulnerable to the departing shadow of its smile.

Good Smiles Make Friends,
Good Friends Make Smiles.

All smiles eventually leave
anonymous lonely lips
fallen to silent chaos.

The longer a smile remains hidden
in the realm of fantasy
the more likely lips will obsess
with the fear of expressing it.

Hairy wolf lips could chill a smile suddenly
with a spell to the very burning gates of hell.

Like Music On Your Face

Hurried breathless smile with
suckling lips stumbling over each other.

Soft yellow light spilling across
young pushed open lips brought shivering
vivid memory of a long nose witch's
crinkled damp nested tight-shut smile
clung with a dry dusty gentle snore.

Hungered restless smile suddenly flared
with revolting incessant rising tides
of ghastly pleasure seeking lips.

✲

Beyond touching and kissing lips is
the silent voice of a smile.

✲

Smiles Don't Like Solitary Confinement.
Set One Free.

✲

Red lips come into this black world
to attain the perfect white light of enlightenment.

Reflections on a Smile

Learn well that the limits of power have no authority
near a drunken smile tended by blood stained lips.

Black magic is when a smile becomes the ghost of lips.

Hot fat lips spanned tight across clear cool cheeks
parading with a rubbery reckless smile
is a rare freaking phenomenon.

Murmuring lips shifting into a swelling roar of
impatience strain and choke at leashed smile.

Decrepit dark creeping lips begin to sink in
over spread cracked teeth each lanterned with a
barely glowing pulsating gelatinous smile.

Tricked-out lips self-congratulating
a brainless smile decaying at its core.

Every Great Smile Is A
Purification Of The World.

Like Music On Your Face

Silken lips waiting for you, quite still,
not waisting only wishing for
a long-lived summer smile.

Bubbling smile crooned
the prettiest song ever heard through pink petal lips
gentler than a whimpering choir of treasured angels.

Unutterable lips possessed with
the tormented smile of blazing rage.

Still lips echoed with a faint smile after
tearing away from a lover's sinking heart
cursing one last note into the darkened wind.

It's hard to smile with love
when one's lips are broken, heartbroken,
happiness ended, existence disintegrated,
all there isn't will never be.

A smile permanently tied to overbearing lips
is painfully wanting to become free of ownership.

Reflections on a Smile

※

So you believe that your feeling heart
lays concealed within every pore of your lips
and like unearthing a dig your inner smile
can be painstakingly uncovered?

※

Intelligence Is The Invisible
Latticework Of The Human Body And
Wisdom Expresses Itself Through A Smile.

※

Her virgin lips had serendipitously discovered
they were capable of transmitting a
sexually virtuous smile.

※ ※

The passion of a smile takes on the flower of its lips.

※ ※ ※

His stranded desperate lips.
carried a heavy smile
cloaked with a veneer of nausea.

※ ※ ※ ※

She resurrected his haunting lips
by spinning a web of silky sinews
recycled from a living smile of black tissue
clinging under the charcoal black nose
of a parasite infested half-skeleton.

Like Music On Your Face

✺ ✺ ✺

A smile takes a trip beyond the frontier of lips
into the secret galaxy of love.

✺ ✺

Dream of moon-glow
patterning a smile on grateful curved lips

✺

His buttered tongue licked a layer or two of dust off a
smile whose part-closed lips shook with laughter.

✺

A Face Without A Smile Is Like
A Body Without A Soul.

✺

The victim identified the suspect as having stark white
porcelain clad teeth shrieking in their bony sockets
chattering around an inner court carpeted by a
struggling heaving tongue all gated with great closed
solid lips canted with a drunken stumbling smile.

✺ ✺

Stunned lips instantly sensed
without outwardly showing something amiss
with a once vowed "I love you" smile.

Reflections on a Smile

❋ ❋ ❋

Dreamlike lips pulsate a
rhythm of unexpected smiles.

❋ ❋ ❋ ❋

When a beautiful smile leaves a room
there's some floating essence of it
that remains on my lips.

❋ ❋ ❋

Lips so numb with false smiles
preached by a red-eyed devil on judgement Sunday.

❋ ❋

God-like lips are always lonely and hungry
without a delicious smile nestled on breast.

❋

Even if you only think of a smile
without the slightest quiver of your lips it takes
momentum from the footprints of your past.

❋

A Smile Does Not Fly On The Wings Of Inevitability.
It Flies On The Spirits Of Those Who Are
Willing To Be In Harmony With Nature.

Like Music On Your Face

A dark smile shrouded in withered lips
musters enough bile to propagate so lips can replicate.

Lips have only so much intimacy.
Their smile penetrates every open pore like
incense intoxicating every sense with
an invisible disappearing plume.

✣ ✤ ✣

Poor charred lips begging pain relief
salve with a futile suffocating smile.

✣ ✤ ✣ ✤

A disturbing arraignment of lips spelled with hunger
homing for a homesick smile.

Lips snapped a fierce stricken smile
like striking a match.

Bad directions could get lips lost in an incomplete smile.

✤

A ghastly smile vomited from hole-studded
sinister lips covered with an effluvia of
mud crusted dead leaves and insects.

Reflections on a Smile

✻

A True Clear Smile Dispels All Misfortune
And Instills The Pure Light
Of Purification Into Worthy Lips.

❦

Shy lips reached out to each other
over the bridge of a gravitational smile.

❦ ❦

A smile is not about the lips.
It emerges from dreams.

❦ ❦ ❦

A time comes when a smile has to divorce its lips,
reject the unbearably luscious memory of what was
in order to hunt drunk the source of its imagination.

❦ ❦ ❦ ❦

Itinerant lips with smiles hungry for hearts to eat.

❦ ❦ ❦

A jagged smile trimmed with torn and broken lips.

❦ ❦

A smile created by some mysterious alchemy of
lips rubbed with an herbal mixture of analgesic balm
and finely powdered unbridled enthusiasm.

Like Music On Your Face

❊

Stare into a smile long and deep.
Let yourself be drawn into its red hot brazier lips.

❊

Fixing Your Smile Issues
Could Give You the Edge You Need.

❊

Lips that blur and shiver as a blazing violet shadow
escape death with the familiar touch
of a warm radiant smile.

❊ ❊

Grave-dug lips had an outgrowth of miniature tubers
that reincarnated into a flora of smiling tulips.

❊ ❊ ❊

Lips lure you with a seductive smile
that can seize your will.

❊ ❊ ❊ ❊

From deep within the dank caves of
childhood gifts withheld we knew the giddy lips
but couldn't retrieve the lost smiles.

❊ ❊ ❊

Torched smile reflected flared lips
tossed onto the creature's skinned face.

Reflections on a Smile

A guru's smile is like a dancing scimitar
chopping off double standard lips, shattering egos
into tiny needles of splintered me, myself, I and mine.

If our lips fail us then all disappointments
are disappointments of smiles.

Life's Perfect Circle Exists
In The Meeting Of A Smile And Frown.

Purple lips devoured each other's dreaded loneliness,
like to like, a horrible dark web
sickened with loneliness.

Brutal lips behave wickedly toward a smile.

A smile with whispering transparent lips
echoing faint wisps of strange drifting dreams.

Sudden miracle of a flaming smile
burst out of a sparked hot licking tongue
leaping against dry crackling lips.

Like Music On Your Face

Cadaverous lips slept with a smile of remorse
…ever, ever, never.

A smile is only meant to keep conversation spinning
while lips search for words to waltz with.

Old weary thin lips strangely sweating with a sickness
that could cough a smile inside out.

Happiness Is Anywhere You Happen To Be—
With Good Health, Good Company, Bright Smile,
And A Fat Burger Between Your Lips.

Feral lips marked their territory
with a pinpoint smile.

What are lips without a smile
but a hollow vessel waiting to be filled?

Love burns with a jet flame starred smile
painted on a face scarred as white as winter snow.

Reflections on a Smile

⁕ ⁕ ⁕ ⁕

Passionate lips trill and
flush silent wandering winds of love;
spent smile's work is done.

⁕ ⁕ ⁕

When puberty first glimpses a virgin smile
it becomes an unforgettable instant enslavement,
an eternal infatuation with succulent lips.

⁕ ⁕

Suitor's lips waged warrior smiles
hoping to stalk and stun his object of love
with gentle piercing cupid arrows,
so many shaft tips in the sky
that the shooter became lost in the
battle cloud with loved one annoyed.

⁕

Lips have a penchant for wasted behavior,
easy smiles followed by vituperous stabs.

⁕

A Nutritional Smile
Stimulates the Release Of Love Hormones
And Relationship Growth Factors.

⁕

The joy of a smile is released from the heart,
rises up the throat until lips shine wet
with living ecstasy of heart and flesh.

An abyss of famished smiles whose lips
might as well have been amputated with
nothing behind them but dwindling corpses.

Blazing lips grew hotter with
every instinct jungled smile.

Her smile went blank into oblivion after
drunk lips were overcome with spinning glee.

Tragic lips gradually changed their waning smile
from faded to disappeared.

Her red lips caught fire into an
awe-filled glowing smile.

Exhausted lips shook to the very core
by thunder-like forces within the
quaking rumbling half-spent inverse smile.

Increase Your Smile Energy Naturally
With A Breakfast Of Love And Lips To Go.

The most perfect lips were always those still smiling.

Her smile brimming with laughter and scented roses brings delight and joyful lips singing to any occasion.

Banal lips require no work at all except to maintain a fictional smile from indifferent scrutiny.

Lips draw your attention like gravity but the smile is the inescapable dark matter of one's being.

Devotional lips tantalized with the lifelong longing for a genuine unknowable smile, a supernatural experience.

Increase Your Smile Energy

A very peaceful place—meditating on the
emotions rendered by a flowering smile,
like ruby smoke rising over pale petals.

Heartfelt smiles are already making love
long before spontaneous lips smack with voltage.

A Downturned Smile Is
The Leading Cause Of Disease.

Take caution if formless lips leap
a swift fierce smile onto your face.

Red flowering lips crowned a
younger smile in the making
regretfully looking away from the dark grave.

Once lips have tasted a smile they can
never completely quit the drug of desire,
the multifaceted diamond of power,
the perils of forbidden love,
the writhing snake of self-deceit.

Reflections on a Smile

How is it that plain dumb and simple lips
never tire in resolve to seek a Nobel Smile?

Electric lips surged with heart-stopping true grit
too stubborn for their own good do die for smiles.

All a smile has to do is grab some lips
with invisible jazz and go for broke.

Enchanted lips smile and send out bursts of love
aromatic with rich sweet rose juice.

A Sad Lazy Smile Is A
Major Risk Factor For Poor Health.

For a smile there is no pillow in the world
as rich and sumptuous as peaceful
sleeping lip-kissed pouching cheeks.

Cold lips heavy with death seemed an
unforgivable down payment for a sweet smile
released into the clouds of heaven.

Increase Your Smile Energy

※ ※ ※

His intense unbearable smile
was buttressed by steely-web lips
creeping ceaselessly inside an inaudible scream.

※ ※ ※ ※

Her wounded lips were bathed and kissed
with a fragrant steamy smile.

※ ※ ※

Determined lips fled from slavery formed a smile
for better or worse to be reborn into the gift of liberty.

※ ※

Two nimble lips watching each other's
sketches of love enhanced smiles.

※

Lips crying out in delirium of fever thirst for more than
a riddling smile from a confounded novice healer.

※

The Cure For All Disease Is
An Injection Of An Authentic Smile.

※

Rare is the worn out old man
that dies with a smile on his lips.

Reflections on a Smile

※ ※

Drunken stumbling turned away smile
seeped with icy chill numbing lips
stiff and frightened against the sharp sword
piercing into a tangled cobweb of dark merciful cries.

※ ※ ※

A sensual smile sweeps downward over the
delicate shape of an upper lip and
circles perfectly around its puffed lower sibling.

※ ※ ※ ※

In the transformation of life
lips lose their meaning and every smile
is reincarnated into a new spirit.

※ ※ ※

Lips choose to leave a relationship
without leaving a trace
of even an imagined smile.

※ ※

Your first smile, then your first lips,
then your first light-headed feeling,
then your first stomach swirl as if a Disney coaster
drops 1000 feet without warning,
then your first love, your first confusion,
discord erupts, then your second smile, then again.

Increase Your Smile Energy

A furious bitter smile arose from the
dense stormy lisp between his lips.

A Saintly Smile Vaccinates You
Against All Harm.

Slimy lips don't care if
an over zealous toilet-smile throws up its stink.

Smile gently quivers as wild dark drink
cloaks mocking lips to restful sleep.

A smile that blooms from soft sounding lips
spreads delight left and right.

A thick honeycomb, even oily, smile
floated above dense and sluggish lips.

A blossom of girly lips leaves
a rose scented smile in the air.

Reflections on a Smile

Lost smile with all strength and resistance
out of its once overpowering lips now
bearing dark ill bitter smells of purification.

Glorious lips are key to
the unseen presence of an alchemical smile.

For A Beautiful Smile,
Let Someone Kiss It Each Day

Fire-stick burned through lips
shed a sick splintered smile dying all over again.

White hot luxurious lips suddenly electrified
into the cold shock of a flint dark smile.

Some smiles go around
trying to get their lips baptized.

She was pure as a snow white smile
painted with freckled lips.

Increase Your Smile Energy

Lips sound pleasant but a smile brings peace.

A smile is the actor on stage
while lips are the audience enjoying it.

Lips cannot be set apart from their smile
or the holiness will not be perceived.

For An Authentic Attractive Smile,
Whisper Words Of Kindness

Drowsy lips listen to the breeze of a smile.

There's a real satisfaction in the thought
of an immortal smile arising from mortal lips.

The feelings in a smile
are never really expressed from the lips.

Love in a smile is a disease no lips can cure.

Reflections on a Smile

Sweltering lips kept awake by
broad memories of beauty and tranquility.

The day you begin to search out
what others see in your smile
will be the last day one ever passes your lips.

A hawkish smile hooded with slashed lips
and uncurling channels of foaming blood sweat.

A Beautiful Smile Is Like A Rainbow,
You Don't Always See It
But The Potential Is Always There.

Lips are a magnificent creation because
they expose a smile with miraculous expression.

Muted lips became so severely lost in a world
where the natural law of real smiles
had never become a wordless language.

Increase Your Smile Energy

A mere quiver detected in the right corner of her lips
struck a smile dumb with engagement.

Hot droopy lips can hardly breathe under the stifling
drugged fertile rhythm of a faintly perfumed smile.

Lips of ruby-like flame maintain
the center of the universe in ecstasy beyond which
there is the complete void—the mystic smile.

A disappointed smile separates the pair of lips
waiting for the right moment.

Behind the smoothness of dull lips
lies a hidden smile growing with magic.

Start Your Healing Journey Today.
Use Your Smile To Heal Yourself And Others
By Harnessing The Proven Power Of Your Smiling Lips
To Assist With Physical And Mental Pain.

Reflections on a Smile

All lips are different—their shape,
plumpness, pucker, color, texture—
with no choice but to touch you
with an infinitely sexual sea of smile.

Disoriented lips liberated an emerging gale
of abandoned hallucinating smiles.

A proud smile unchained, ferocious, doing battle against
more graceful better natured Olympian strength lips.

Lips dripping with the murky tongue of
an old leather hound cocked in a deathtrap smile.

A web of disaster tangles in a heartbeat
when ruddy lips turn slowly into a red star
spinning wildly into a smiling black night.

A famous smile is a cherished secret,
a disguise removing the true identity
of a man's character from the competition.

Increase Your Smile Energy

Switched on lips have an invisibility factor
which allows its stealth smile to
penetrate any living space of interest or desire.

A Natural Smile Is Nature's Gift For Health.

When lips stare down into the truth of a smile
a thunderous revelation strips away a secret world
of pure silence.

Lips on fire bring pleasurable smiles as fleeting as smoke.

Whiskey wet lips
blurred with nostalgia of coital paradise,
swaying beds, rhythmic locking,
shamanic singing, thrusting hips,
thrashing arms, sensuous smiles;
everywhere beauty entwined with grotesque.

Lips follow conventions of genetics and evolution but
smiles are a wide open gift not responding to god-like
wisdom, beyond spiritual and mathematical chaos.

Reflections on a Smile

✻ ✱ ✻

Semiconscious lips drugged with love
risking a smile's annihilation
by a dangerous journey to the edge of eroticism.

✻ ✱

A smile elevates lips. Beyond a smile is love.
True love is fully expressed by death.
Death reincarnates lips, smile and love.

✻

A smile can't be destroyed without killing the lips too.

✱

A Smile Is One Of The Essential Nutrients
That Everyone Needs.

✱

Lips have a centrifugal force which cannot overcome
the centripetal force of a smile.

✱ ✻

Bitter lips disappointed in its smile for not becoming
more than hoped for, as if bound within
a metamorphosing chrysalis paralyzed in time.

✱ ✻ ✱

Soft young lips were quenched with a cool mystical
charm as if numbing cold water still rippling from
a shaded pebble dropping to endless dark depths.

Increase Your Smile Energy

Dripping wet beautiful lips
distilling weakness and pettiness
out of an iconic smile.

The death of a smile
is due to circumstances beyond control of the lips.
It's done, zero, should never had been,
beyond vastness, never to be recovered.

Every lip a smile touches
celebrates sexual power
in a game of authentic and fraud.

Can a noble but beaten smile
stay married to bad lips with even worse intention,
neither able to cross the separate worlds they exist in?

※

A Smile Is One Of Nature's
Most Powerful Anti-depressants
That Protects your Emotions From Damage.

Smiles act polite, consent to an encounter, kidnap lips,
and watch out because dumb love will get you busted.

Reflections on a **Smile**

A smile can melt all solids.
What are lips supposed to do, despair?

Lips are human, not god-like,
and the pursuit of godliness is what is called a smile.

A smile hunts for its quarry obsessively
hoping to change its lips into love.

You will never become enlightened if you try
to distinguish whether the lips are real or smile unreal.

Poisoned lips pasted with a deadly mind-control fungus
suddenly urged to unleash a spray of invisible smile dust.

A fragile smile can never be safe
in a perilous world of hostile lips.

❋

Let The Mirror Of Your Heart
Reflect The Success Of Your Smile.

❋

An unfamiliar smile is as lips lost in a foreign country.

❋ ❋

Upper lip teased its lower sibling just as father's tacit not-so-easy completely blank smile fouled forth.

❋ ❋ ❋

Contradicting lips fooled around
with an unbalanced smile.

❋ ❋ ❋ ❋

Shocked lips like a phosphene banner whirling
below a wind swept cumulus nimbus smile.

❋ ❋ ❋

Lips sweet as fleshy figs with divine skin
spit a distasteful venomous smile.

Reflections on a Smile

A smile doesn't reveal its true devotion
until its lips are unfettered.

Foxy lips infested with mirth
flashing ridiculous smiles to and fro
effortlessly like magic.

Be Good To Your Teeth, Your Smile Will Bless You.

Lips taste of gall from a belly wound forcing a bitter
angry colorless and passionless punishing smile.

Mistaken voluble lips may appear stupid
but really commune on a spiritual level
with the smiles of divine angels.

A smile that denounces its lips bears a darker shadow
than three moons orbiting over a black forest.

The most romantic thing her smile ever did
was to inflame hot lips to a white heat
and then drench them with rushed cold sex.

The Success Of Your Smile

※ ※ ※

You can't erase a smile?
Try rubbing thorny skinned lips
against his deepest intimate pleasure.

※ ※

Crazy in love lips triumphed into
an ecstatic smile of perfect fulfillment.

※

When your lips have no place else to go,
feel lucky you still can have gratitude in a smile.

※

A Pure Instinctive Smile Strong With Solid Teeth
Is The Fountain Of Youth.

※

She crushed his smile now reaching out
from beyond a bleeding death,
lips clawing and aching with impending doom.

※ ※

Anguished lips understood that a false smile
promising to return is even more devastating
than its potential to live on forever.

Reflections on a **Smile**

※ ※ ※

Despairing death loomed near
but could be vanquished if only his lips were raised
enough to celebrate her unfulfilled smile.

※ ※ ※ ※

A soaring smile in paradise has a splendid view
of its ten thousand chanting lips.

※ ※ ※

An intimate sighting unveils her lips
to become visible in shape and texture
with their secret smile inviting my cast down eyes.

※ ※

A smile is never final even though
it seems complete in itself
because in the background lips have a compulsion
for miracles of an infinite variety of love.

※

An exalting smile, more often than not,
is not what earthly yearning lips deserve.

※

Tough Times Call For Tender Smiles.

The Success Of Your Smile

Silent smiles burst from sweet-talking lips,
swindling bandits anticipating imaginary pleasures
in hidden places behind a perfumed mask.

Tight lips went into delicate convulsions
before swallowing a smile saltier than oysters.

Lips said you were the most beautiful smile
in the world, my Cleopatra, sultry music,
naked beating rhythm of my dreams,
every desire ever wanted…and on.

Lips enjoyed a sucked up banquet
of clear cerebrospinal fluid from his straw-like
spiny tailbone to brainstem like an imploding urchin
swimming in a sea of fantastic smiles.

A dazzling smile is a surreal window
through which the unconscious mind can peer into
and amplify the true character of fleshy lips.

Reflections on a Smile

No need to rub away any stubble on cheek and chin
once lips burnish a smile
under the nose of a lighthearted gent.

Life Is Better When Your Smile Is At Your Best

Use of one's lips as weapons
is born into every savage smile.

Lips sometimes have a strange sense
that a smile shouldn't exactly reflect
the deepest sincerity behind its subtle meanings.

At last a sensual smile will follow its mummified lips into
the grave and beyond
burying passions…poof…slumbered carnal desires.

A warm inward turning smile
kept lingering on lips of past contentment,
weary with age old memory.

The Success Of Your Smile

⁂

Lips in an altered state can suddenly become unnerved
by the possibility of a smile losing all moorings
and drifting unpredictably with a spirit of revenge
into a parallel universe.

⁂

Starry white lips shiver back blistering cold
blizzard winds weighing steadily
against the slow tide of a spring smile.

⁂

Never fear. Lips are a transitional phase,
a trite annoyance soon supplanted by a smile
bursting through our fabric of ordinary vision,
no trick involved but a powerful dizzy manifestation
breaching all outside rules.

✻

A Smile Should Always Have Enough Energy
To Look As If It Could Spark the World

⁂

Life sprang into the stone still smile
and in an instant blood warm sweet lips
thumped a pulse against my breast.

Reflections on a Smile

Surging lips responded to a caress of a smile by
spilling out the corners a divine nectar of great love.

Lips looked beyond the smile and witnessed
an unseen twilight zone, an irradiating melt-down
of yesterday fears knowing that
what once was slipping into magic is now reality.

Hurrying lips with swiftly changing emotions
storming over a last billow of a lover's turmoiled smile.

A fantasy smile can damage ordinary lips and bind them
to mystical dreams of an unknown future.

Butterfly red raspberries lips innocent and believing
with purity and right intention can disarm
the shameful spirit right out of your smile.

An absolute smile offers a full opening of the lips,
total unrestrained honesty.

❇

The Best Smiles Have A Mix
Of Warm Heart and Cool Pleasures

⁕

Yellow white lips fronted the smiling gateway,
chess-like assembled ivory teeth worthy
of fighting for victory over Queen's black.

⁕ ⁕

Lipsomania. Smilorama.
Everything in excess in triumphantly naked self-love.

⁕ ⁕ ⁕

Naked steel sword dangerously trapped
between battling lips and royal teeth
with deliberate intent to strike down blasphemy.

⁕ ⁕ ⁕ ⁕

An ethereal smile emanates from mortal lips
much as the psychic energies of angel stars
influence the formulaic lives of the human zodiac.

Reflections on a Smile

※ ※ ※

Startled widening smile suddenly stripped
of ragged lips smothered in feverish hate.

※ ※

Pair of loving lips melting through and through
until there was nothing left but the
memory of the flavor of a smile of ecstasy.

※

Wanton lips exorcised of paranormal
haunting smiles, deserted angels
in immortal liaison with gleaming demons.

※

A Bright Smile Elevates Any Celebration

※

An unfulfilled smile is like an amputated phantom lip,
still twitching pretending to breathe and chant,
not yet aware that it's streaming a life energy force.

※ ※

Helpless smile fatally strangled
in a tangled bite of demonic lips.

※ ※ ※

Hers was a secret smile that had nothing to do
with the rhythmic dancing of wild lips.

A Mix Of Warm Heart And Cool Pleasures

The musical tones of his smile made
unutterable words a new language for shy lips.

The greatest joy in a smile comes
when lips are freed from life's burdens.

Lips tire, perspire, run out of breath
but a smile is liquid speed with an otherworld
blurry excitation of indefatigable energy.

❋

With these lips I give you my smile.
With this smile I renounce thy lips.

❋

Sometimes The Road To Happiness
Isn't A Road At All But More A Prescription:
One Smile Twice A Day.

❋

A mocking smile, fake in most ways,
is as dull as overly dry cement with cracks
where guilty lips might slide into and hide.

Reflections on a Smile

In a blink lips moved apart
smiling into a long-gapped pause of hollow words.

Lips with high moral conceit are often
leaking with disappointment in their smile's
constant inept short-fallings.

Enduring feather beaked scavengers had attended
to everything but the gradual wasting of a
thick fleshy smile drawn with yellowing beastly lips.

Lunatic lips seize with epileptic smiles
that were assessed, diagnosed and prescribed
to be bloodlessly crucified with chemical drugs.

A smile deep within the throat cast a ritual spell
tearing asunder spellbound drunk lips.

Love struck lips painfully puffed up and choking
with restrained flirting smiles rising slowly,
losing control then lightening burst into
flying flames of psychotic passion.

❋

In Any Town Or City That You Go To,
The Thing That Makes It Special
Is The Smile Of The People.

❋

Deadly evil lips spawned a devouring howling smile
as though one was a shadow of the other.

❋ ❋

Lips search deep within their heart
and ask from where the spirit smile becomes.

❋ ❋ ❋

The first lips you touch and open up to love
are forever imagined in your dreams
as pillow clouds of smiles.

❋ ❋ ❋ ❋

Lips can never recapture a smile once released
no more than an embryo can unwind
to its essential separate parts of DNA.

Reflections on a Smile

Quiet lips lingering above in cloud chambers were
hunted and destroyed by the gravity of a captive smile.

Her classic smile was a magnet
drawing pulsating lips of genuflecting patrons,
great men conspiring scandals in naked dreams.

The worst of smiles is burning
in the lips of banished devils.

Reflect Your Own Personal Inner Smile

Misbehaving lips forbade a distressed smile
as if dismissing a used lover.

Lips seemed to float under a whiskered smile.

A half-smile vibrating impotent and insane
in a catch lip gravity field unwilling to trust
in its auto determinant self-power.

The Smile Of The People

A smile is like a faucet with taps for hot and cold lips.

Only a smile can know
the true spirit of its original lips.

Lips rank as an old cloth soaked in gasoline hummed a
smile like a turbocharged black German roadster.

You can't fix your curiosity on the bare essential of a smile
and understand the intimacy your lips sense.

*

Who Wears It Better—
A Fashionable Fake Empty Outer White Smile
Or A Healthy Sensual Inner Smile?

Straining lips trembling and untouched,
hesitating yearning for a naked smile of love.

If only an educated pair of lips could secret
the destiny of a smile, maybe foreshadow its madness.

Reflections on a Smile

Grateful lips gave back a loving smile that had been
gathered through an era of peace, containment, kinships.

Cold lips on the edge of disaster
kiss a warm fleshed smile.

For some plaster lips a smile is not
something to look forward to as they would
rather not peel the skin off a tragic story.

The ego of lips always deserving gratitude lives lost in the
shadow of smile's wonderment miracles.

Lips were made primarily for smiling
but kissing is tinsel on the tree.

You Know You're A Grown-Up
When You Nurture Your Inner Smile
To Brighten Your Outer Smile.

Salmon-like rubbery lips unfurling a great white sail
of a smile plotted precisely with a compass of love.

The Smile Of The People

Puny lips can't ever provoke nor humble
a smile that has majesty on an
unimaginable scale of wonderment.

A dark cold heart crippled with deflated lips
that slumped and surrendered with a moaning smile.

Lips are born with a genetic blueprint
of "x" smiles per lifetime and each smile
splits apart the lips, keeps dividing and dissecting them
until the original intent becomes reflected.

Half-heard muttering of lost copper lips
flickering uncertain but inevitable odd smiles.

A sweet smile itched for freedom
from her restless lips.

Beautiful lips once seemed so fresh and full of passion
now only a whisper of a smile
dimmed with suffering wrapped in death cloth.

Reflections on a Smile

✽

It's Not How You Smile,
It's How Your Smile Glows!

❊

Evil genius cursing his smile, forbidding his
wickedly tipped tongue from wetting his raw lips.

❊ ❊

What should intimate lips do
with such an elegant smile?

❊ ❊ ❊

Lips like a photograph have an objective finite ending
but a smile burns personal feeling
into the infinite soul of timelessness.

❊ ❊ ❊ ❊

Recognize saintly lips by the sea
of calm smile around them
drowning you in ohm peace.

❊ ❊ ❊

Suddenly lips became hot iced and the frozen smile
shattered into diamond powdered dust.

❊ ❊

A mysterious smile of waiting lips
dancing in the stillness of a living circle's potency.

The Smile Of The People

※

Cold pinched lips choked by their own frigid smile.

※

A Smile That Is Anything But Ordinary
Can Bring Human Aging To A Standstill.

※

Extraordinary lips that seemed to express a smile
magnified by innocent passion.

※ ※

The colors of a smile are fading everywhere,
perfect twisted overlapped maze of emotions gushing
into the verge of collapse, shot lips dropped dead.

※ ※ ※

Sunset red lips lay limp and dead with privileged glory
knowing they were no less significant a badge
against a frightful ghosts's smile.

※ ※ ※ ※

Black mournful lips dripping with green spit of hate.

※ ※ ※

Squatted lipped old toothless smile
beckons you obscenely with its cracked crooked tongue.

61

Reflections on a Smile

※

A sky clouded thunderclap fury of suffering smiles
was dismantled by mucous drooling diseased lips.

※

Lips are born discreetly away from public scrutiny
in nocturnal biochemistry pulsing through
millions of singing vessels, veins and arteries
while a smile's passion soars into extremely public
spaces seeking infinite perpetuations.

※

A Smile Can Work Miracles,
But Unfortunately You Can't Keep One Up All Day.

※

Smiles don't make judgements
nor enter into disputes that lips would twist and
bend into traps in your head.

※

Robust lips have an earthly power but a smile in love
reveals its true capacity only when it declares infidelity.

※

The thug had a slow long smile of chafed lips
swearing with raw rubbed wool.

The Smile Of The People

Lips know every mystery
except the incomprehensible smile.

Enjoy a wonderfully happy smile with quiet calm lips.

Deadly cursing smile of leach rooted lips
burning with venom.

The softness of her lips was measured
against the harmony of her smile.

Search The World For A Better Smile
And Break Through To The Other Side.

A dazzling evening smile begins its day with morning
flickering sleepy lips awakened as glowing embers.

The evolution of lips is a strange portrait.
One can never predict from a sketch
the various stirrings of its smile.

Reflections on a Smile

Lips are master of reality in both physical and sensual
worlds. A smile can touch a kiss only in a fantasy dream.

Lips curled up burst with thunderous fierce heat
and swelled into a divine arched smile.

Lips in a terrible state
tired of being alone without a smile.

Ridiculous lips try to lisp a smile
into an interesting thought.

A smile has no great assurance
that it will be comforted by cordial lips.

❋

Amp Up Your Smile Power With 32
Healthy Sharp Teeth Of White Pearl Enamel,
Solid Bone And Firm Gums—
The Original Smile Booster.

❋

Mean lips can knock down a timid smile
with enough kick to make a sandstone cry.

❋ ❋

In the distance behind the haze of a dizzy smile
appeared a mirage of screaming lips.

❋ ❋ ❋

Glowing pale orange lips obscured
by the magic arousal of a luminous smile.

❋ ❋ ❋ ❋

Thrashing lips sucking into a sickly blue tint
waiting for the cool crystal smile of death.

❋ ❋ ❋

A black scaled tongue licked his loathsome lips
clean of its lustful smile.

Reflections on a Smile

Can a single pair of lips shower a glitter of smiles
like water droplet diamonds?

Shivering miserable lips
released the absolute darkness of the creature's smile.

Smiling Lips And Sharp Teeth
Have The Miracle Power To Promote The Good
And Banish The Bad

Her lips were sweaty with a clinging unwelcome desire
to acid wash his cruel ungrateful smile.

When a smile hits you hard
everything becomes still with perfect silence,
your lips lose all sense of where they are
and what they're doing.

He wore a smile with hounding lips
whipping the truth like a snake with two tails.

The Original Smile Booster

The last standing warrior left with a battered nose
clinging to a crooked cut smiling upper lip
waving like ribbons flung in a cheer.

The profound essential voice of a smile
is to sing the music of lips
into the expanding universe.

Perfectly good but old lips in a lonesome smile.

Of the two a friend's smile is the greater mystery
than a stranger's lips.

Your Smile Your Brain And Your Heart
Can Conquer America's Dysfunctional
Love Affair With White Teeth.

Blasphemous bitter lips could sting
and suck rotting nectar out of any smile.

A smile can make poor lips much more than they are.

Reflections on a Smile

⁂

Every single smile is a flowering bud
variant from its beautiful rooted lips.

⁂

Precious brushing lips caress
with a smooth flowering lavish smile.

⁂

Black smile stretched lean lips
gashed with a long knife sharp thumbnail.

⁂

Beautiful begging lips struggling for an answering smile.

⁂

Lips templed in splendid silence soon to be broken open
and scattered into myriad vanishing smiles.

✵

A Loving Smile Went Up Against
21st Century's Best Pain Reliever…It Bowled It Over!

⁂

Coveting lips resentful of the smile they want
but can't have.

The Original Smile Booster

✳ ✳

Beauty and misery in a single set of lips
capture the emotional heart of a rose scented smile.

✳ ✳ ✳

A smirk is nothing more than a thin toasted lip
with a shabby smile smeared on it.

✳ ✳ ✳ ✳

Surprised straight lifted lips stirred at one corner
into a thundering fierce smile with prospect for death.

✳ ✳ ✳

Lips smiled at the wrong time
completely ignorant of misplaced words.

✳ ✳

Secret searching lips licked by a torchlight smile.

✳

Crushed lips quivering too wildly
to set a murderous smile.

✳

The Rules Have Changed—
Feel Younger With Every Smile!

Reflections on a Smile

⚘

A terrible nightmare of cold fear hid a silent smile
prowling with smudged mongrel lips.

⚘ ⚘

Christian virgin lips don't lose their fertile smile
without some repressed discomfort.

⚘ ⚘ ⚘

A smile of leisure
will never be supported long by slaving lips.

⚘ ⚘ ⚘ ⚘

Lips pursed against an oily smile
grew foul with sweat and unexpected brutality.

⚘ ⚘ ⚘

Lips are not the smile. Lips are smile-holders
with chameleon control over dream images.

⚘ ⚘

Cold stuttering lips nervously spayed a virgin smile.

⚘

Angry weeping smile distanced
by lips with an unspeakable seriousness.

✽

Only A Smile Can Conquer Aging—
And It's Guaranteed!

❧

Blue and shining ice cold lips
embraced within a fully naked smile
not for love but only for rosy warmth.

❧ ❧

Stunned lips calm and unable to move
because of a momentary cool smile.

❧ ❧ ❧

Black opal lips of hate danced piteously
in the shell of a once magnificent smile.

❧ ❧ ❧ ❧

A smile is such a slight strange thing to be
extinguished by only a simple passing puff of the lips.

❧ ❧ ❧

His smile was parched with lips burned and scarred
holding blank emotionless charred sadness.

Reflections on a Smile

Comforting lips tucked up together
into a slumbering smile.

The blue sky was a perfect canvas for her smile
painted with the instant freshness
of sunlit pink full lips however clumsy in song.

An Awesome Smile Is An Incredible Defeat
If It's Spirit Is Stained With 32 Gnarly Teeth.

Billowing smile fell over deserving lips
like a transforming veil.

Love enchanted lips charmed
by a heavenly scented potion of a sensual smile.

Terror obliterated smile
descended back into its aching lips
with recollections of a menacing devil.

Only A Smile Can Conquer Aging

All the lips on the planet
carry a genetic retrospective judgement
of every smile ever created with a
ridiculously inadequate mechanism to search
into the true meaning behind the source.

Strongly painted army of startled smiles
jumped with a grand glorious blaze of rejoicing
as if their captive lips were ready for more amore.

It is both small and grave things
that inspire lips to pucker into a smile.

Scrunched up lips like a blind squint
spent too much time searching the night
for a smile lost in a dark smokey cloud of espionage.

No One Can Put A Price
On The Treasures Of A Smile.

Shaken lips emitting a dead sound,
then nothing but a threatening dark zombie smile.

Reflections on a Smile

Dense plump lips longed to be crushed experimentally,
like fragrant blossom petals in an aromatherapy lab,
to enjoy the release of a sweet smelling smile.

Smiling dry ribbed lips speckled
with erupted iridescent sores
screamed when painfully rubbed
by his bleeding stump of broken wrist bone.

An upper lip flirting with lower
is the secret success of an irresistible smile.

A flaming smile can turn gloomy lips bright.

Death soon comes to weary lips
when they can no longer smile
with the light of gratitude.

Her painful lips drained away the strength of his smile.

✻

There Are Many Frustrations In Life
But Your Smile Can Overcome All Of Them.

✻

A smile can only imagine an existence without lips
while immersed in a delicate dream.

✻ ✻

An aberration in a smile is about as easy for lips to sense
as daybreak's gradual lightening.

✻ ✻ ✻

The morning sunlight
decomposes everything that bears no shadow
in a structured final way—eyes to ears,
neck to wrists, chest to hips, waist to ankles
—but a smile infects the whole of eternity.

✻ ✻ ✻ ✻

People say your smile is like a screw.
The lips give cause, smile brings effect,
then relax, forget, compress, escape.

Reflections on a Smile

※ ※ ※

Wartorn hungry lips hunted defenseless smiles.

※ ※

Wobbly legs propped up a partied smile deeply lost
in blue-black lips sauced by fruity blackberry wine.

※

He couldn't fire up a smile hot enough
to burn the truth into patriotic but disillusioned lips.

※

A Porcelain Created Smile
Is The Greatest Illusion Of Our Time.

※

Lips with a vague blur of a naked cold smile
were colored by a reflected winter pale icy blue sky.

※ ※

A lavish smile calls attention
to ordinary lips in excess of themselves.

※ ※ ※

A thousand kisses by your lips
resonates with a dream of a
never to be forgotten ever loving smile.

Your Smile Can Overcome Frustrations

Lips orbiting the secret space of her flower
with a perfectly weightless smile
is the greatest pleasure in the world.

Death kissed by a murderous smile
with electrical lips of metallic foil.

Heavy muscle of lips pounded
a sledge hammer fist of emotion
into a smile that had more stink than
freshly laid sticky hot black top asphalt.

Arid crackling lips groaned into a cramped smile
of sex starved migraines and marbled gall stones.

Money Can't Buy A "Natural" Smile.

Snake-like lips bear forth a new smile
from their molted dead lifeless skin.

Ghost white smile with scarcely noticed lips
void of even a shadow of substance.

Reflections on a Smile

Everyone has brushed a lip with a smile
but to kiss one with magnified purpose
is to consecrate its Divine Nature.

In a glimpse of light all the smiles
were about nothing but lips thirsty for truth.

What a thousand matter-of-fact lips
wouldn't give for one earnest smile.

A lost cave full of abandoned lips
with haunting smiles until death.

Loose lips so nice, soft and firm
had self-induced a serenaded smile.

Brew Smiles With Fresh-Ground Humor
And Make The World's Finest Organic Infusion Grin!

Stumbling bare cold lips not able to negotiate
a black cursed smile for the witch's brew.

Your Smile Can Overcome Frustrations

※ ※

Lips can be desirable but their smile undesirable
or lips can be undesirable with a desirable smile
plus an infinite number of variations in the moment.

※ ※ ※

Youthful lips are deeply attracted
to worldly love and desire so they rub hard
the smile in a bottle to enliven the genie within.

※ ※ ※ ※

Lips may stop feeling but the smile never forgets.

※ ※ ※

Troubled times discouraged many smiles
with lips half mournful and half furious.

※ ※

His proud smile, clean and white with expression, was
called out disrespectfully by stained and yellowed lips.

※

Artist smile snap-punched with an array
of needled lip studs to pain-up the right brain.

※

A Natural Smile
Is Nature's Gift For Health.

Reflections on a Smile

Lonesome lips rest against each other,
as bees touching honey nectar,
pretending the taste of a smile in love with itself.

They coupled with a peaceful smile
in a silent night of invisible lips.

His belly rich smile mustard with delight
a hotly buttered sandwich of lips.

Her passion was to taste a cinnamon smile
drizzled with black licorice lips.

Loving bad lips gains you great reputation
for stealing bankster smiles.

The criminal investigator traced a suspicious smile
as if the lips missed something.

A living smile has a godly permanence
beyond the mortality of lips.

❉

A Smile Is One Of The
Essential Nutrients That Everyone Needs.

❉

Nookie monster shrugged
a hapless smile of milky raped lips.

❉ ❉

There is truth in a smile
that measures the meaning of what the lips say.

❉ ❉ ❉

Dowsing lips with animal greed use a magnetic smile
to search for a suitable consort.

❉ ❉ ❉ ❉

Give me a galaxy of gorgeous lips
and there would still not exist in the universe
a more splendid smile as in your sweet masterpiece.

❉ ❉ ❉

Lips breathed an unexpected
pure instinctive whisper of a smile.

Reflections on a Smile

※

Imagine a light genial smile on the surface
but iron laid misogyny deep in the lattice of his lips.

※

Every sensory pathway in the body
converged into her gashed lip which recopied
a secret broth of a bleeding revengeful smile.

※

A Smile Is One Of Nature's
Most Powerful Anti-depressants
That Protects Your Emotions From Damage.

※

Sun streaked lips arced wide into a taut smile
like a suspension bridge giving birth
through morning mist.

※

You might think he was born with that creepy smile
of inherited reptile skin lips blanketed with
million year old gold flecked crushed egg shells.

※

Stem cells would refuse to recreate
his mysterious shapeless smile born from
the blackness of immortal virgin lips.

A Smile Is A Nutrient Everyone Needs

Easy to be fooled by a boyish smile
that privately practices his fighting lips
to lash out with hacking and stabbing abandon.

An invisible smile was liquefying
in the intense heat of terror driven lips.

Disturbed lips ordained with a force of self-control
sanctified by a daring memory
of a forgiving caressing smile.

All dreamy smiles are delightfully mad,
pondering the mysteries of trusting slumbering lips.

A Down Turned Smile Is The Leading Cause Of Death.

Lips shifted to make a soft yielding comfort
for an innocuous guarded smile.

Side-by-side cheek-to-cheek comparison of fragrant lips
all have subtly different degrees of elusive smiles.

Reflections on a Smile

Graceless lips struggled
to balance a smile between violence and love.

Time for seltzer when an outgassing smile is stopped
by lips pinched together pressing terrific forces double
what an upper lip of quivering hairy feelers can resist.

Aboriginal lips running upslope to a plateaued nose
stumbled into an ancient paleolithic smile.

Hard working lips fleeced of their smile
with over-the-top drudge.

Like a genie escaping from a bottle
a banquet of a smiles took life from exotic lips.

When Your Smile Changes Everything Changes.

Her lips colored with red flowers
on fire as if lightening struck her smile.

A Smile Is A Nutrient Everyone Needs

A smile protects the honor of lips that are affronted.

Lips may bore people for a long time
but an abstract smile has absolute meaning
even if no one understands.

Ordinary lips unable to express a grateful smile
diminish the holiness of terrible pleasures.

Love is a whirlpool of mosaic feelings
innocent lips can't ever escape.

Steel-jacketed lips could go oogling
an artificial intelligence smile.

Lips once again rational separate themselves
embarrassed with their cheap sweaty smile.

✻

Find Out What Brings You Smiles
And Go There.

❀

Lips slowly and carefully store up
enough power in a kiss to enchant any full grown man.

❀ ❀

A smile with capable lips has the power
to both dull and sharpen the senses.

❀ ❀ ❀

Shimmering lips relaxed
and then surrendered fully to
a rainbow of orgasmic smiles.

❀ ❀ ❀ ❀

Arched lips mirror the entrance to a gothic cathedral
wafting an incense filled smile.

❀ ❀ ❀

Perturbed lips welcome sleepy smiles.

What Brings You Smiles

Nothing is as peculiar
as chanting lips trying to dam up
rivulets of mirth pouring into a smile.

A mellow buzz on the lips
comes with a familiar contentment
of a smile minty dreamy with love.

Lips Can Never Be Fraudulent Because
The Idea Of A Smile Exists Only In The Mind.

How can one not love a hushed smile
with soft golden light crisscrossing shy lips?

How do you spark a smile
that has not been expressed for ages
except in the memory of its lips?

Two lips folded against each other,
matching heart pulses,
breathing in the shared halo of a smile.

Reflections on a Smile

Trembling lips scared by a former life
are being reborn with every threatening smile.

He suffered cold pinched lips
choked by their own frigid smile.

She inherited a brilliant set of golden lips,
a treasured smile of incredible wealth.

His ice-burned lips spread thin into a frosty smile.

Beware The Nonchalant Smile
That Can Park Permanent Residence In Your Lips.

She possessed vapid lips that could seemingly
suck unadulterated passion out of a smile.

Her displeasured lips recruited a striking tongue
that could inject high octane truth serum
to induce an unconscious smile.

What Brings You Smiles

Tiny tot's pure heavenly smile
was christened with prayerful lips.

Blind stripped down lips
ready to break the surface of a muddy smile.

A fallen smile cushioned
by a spasm of thinly padded lips.

His big clump of a pretzeled lip
unstrapped a menacing smile.

❋

A rushed smile can be a terrible mistake
with fanatical half-cocked flaring lips.

❋

Anesthetized Lips
Experience Hallucinations Of The Smile.

❋

Her breath sang an inner smile
played against sherbet lacquered lips.

Reflections on a Smile

✤ ✤

Doubtful lips destined to voyage
an enterprise of untested smiles.

✤ ✤ ✤

Psychoanalysis diagnosed my beau
as a liptrovert and it was recommended that he get the
"Liptrovert's Guide To Loving My Smile Slowly."

✤ ✤ ✤ ✤

Ou-la-la-Bamba lips smile and shake with da-rhythm.

✤ ✤ ✤

Under the lips our smiles are all the same,
clinging to memories and hopeful dreams.

✤ ✤

You are a 100 trillion cell body.
Every hour a billion cells stop smiling
and need to be replaced.

✤

His flesh heart tongue
pressing with passion against your white hot lips
turns my smile ice black.

What Brings You Smiles

❋

Fixing Your Smile Issues
Could Give You The Edge You Need.

❋

If our lips fail us then all disappointments
are disappointments of smiles.

❋ ❋

An improvised smile, begun but never finished,
stares at its lips as if meditation alone should
somehow evoke the right colorful intent and
emotion to fulfill the spirit of the occasion.

❋ ❋ ❋

Her lips were hopelessly consumed
with taking an emotion into grip
when all they need is to smile
and exercise surrender to all reason.

❋ ❋ ❋ ❋

Like an athlete on steroids
fearful of being exposed, the tired old smile
was pumping with high resolve
behind burnt out muscled lips.

Reflections on a Smile

※ ※ ※

Lips twisted, colored, thick, strong,
flawless, voluptuous, disturbing and gentle
hinted at the elusive arboreal leafy scent
of an unpremeditated declaration of a smile.

※ ※

The intensity of my ridiculous smile,
even as her heated lips swept me deeper
into a drowning flood of eager love,
blundered dangerously close to fondling erotic panic.

※

His crushing predatory naked lips blotted out
past memories of pleasures mounting into a hanging
arched smile complicated with frenzied lust and tears.

※

Your Smile,
So Beautiful And Meaningful,
Won't Hatch Out Of A Fortune Cookie.
Free Your Lips Today
And Transform Your Inner And Outer Self
Into An Evolution Of Art And Health.

❋

Yellow Or White Teeth, Red Or Blue Lips.
It Doesn't Matter Because
Everything Goes With A Smile.

❋

Her damp lips fluttered artfully above my swollen smile
ignorant of what lay beneath the trapdoor of conscience.

❋ ❋

Lips can boast only one thing—
a smile get one shot straight to target, out of sight,
not knowing if or where it lands.

❋ ❋ ❋

Is it ridiculously naive for infatuated lips to be
in love with an unknown surrogate sprung smile?

❋ ❋ ❋ ❋

One can't say by the lips whether the
emotions are real or merely paraded manufacturing
but a true smile penetrates to the core
and unmasks itself irrevocably in timeless eternity.

Reflections on a Smile

A smile has that indefinable quality that mere lips
can't impart and only an open heart might discover.

I tasted her lips; she inhaled my smile.
Both of us dropped confused, near destroyed
by erotic aching intimacy, black pitch hair,
silk padded pillow, lunatic passion.

A Shy Smile Holds Deeply Sensual Voltage
Dangerous To Chaste Lips

Lips should never contemplate
the sweetness of a smile until after its execution
at which time a bit of doctoring is called for
to treat riled irrational emotions.

Would a smile be lonely because it became
separated from its lips without knowing why?

Those three words sung so often by lips, "I Love You",
can make the earth move, but a smitten smile bakes
sweetbread for all the angels in the Kingdom of Heaven.

Everything Goes With A Smile

His lips were tranquil and detached, a safe place
where a smile perched on a deer velvet suede zafu
can watch thoughts float through the mind's eye.

Some people feel as fish trapped in an aquarium
with lips pushed against the glass, but a smile
can knock, shake, crash, and flash through every barrier
made by man except one's own perception of reality.

His lips immediately broke into a sweat,
stumbling out of an awkward smile
the new mother-in-law tried to turn on like a tap.

Pity those whose life experience brings them
toiling hard lips and tragic everyday smile.

❋

Stare At A Smile Long Enough And
In Its Reflection You Might See Your Lips
Puppeteered By Anonymous Love.

❋

My smile lived for the memory of my tongue licking
graham crumbs and jelly jewels off his kiddish lips.

Reflections on a Smile

※ ※

A smile is both the cause and cure for love.
Its implanted energetic seed has infinite permanence and,
like a scalpel, it can excise the physical manifestation.

※ ※ ※

He deftly disarmed the attacker with a malicious blow
that smashed through lips, teeth, nose, and brain stem,
lastly, with wicked pleasure sliced his smile off
with a sign of a cross from chin to eyes, ear to ear.

※ ※ ※ ※

Lips are anxious to create the right sweet impression
with fresh energy that powers the love in a smile.

※ ※ ※

He ran his lips and fingertips over her cool flat belly,
up between the valley of her small breasts, and
suddenly couldn't feel or remember who she was;
the barbed poison had finally targeted his basic tactile
senses and her young resplendent smile shimmered
through the nauseating fog of a half drunk memory.

※ ※

The devil poked me trying to overpower my lips
impassioned with her clutching smile.

Everything Goes With A Smile

❊

Her lips smiled at me thick with love
and my endorphins came swimmingly
lost in a gelatinous swish of hope and reality.

❊

A Smile Can't Live By Rules So It Has The Power
To Empty Each And Every One.

❊

When lips observe the spectacle of a perfect smile
they wonder if they ever had
the slightest recognition of any kind of god.

❊ ❊

My lips flapped like a cheap aileron
wildly out of control on a stupidly smiling RC plane.

❊ ❊ ❊

Lips were beguiled by the tiniest of a smile
too quick to lie pinned down.

❊ ❊ ❊ ❊

He entered the room with a switched on smile
toggled to high beam, protected by an upper,
too feminine, roly-poly lip draped over
with curved feather touch black lashes.

Reflections on a Smile

❦ ❦ ❦

Lips tight as a coiled boa around a trapped smile
sought refuge from the painful knot with a warm sherry,
hot buttered toast, and a steamy kiss.

❦ ❦

One of the most beautiful smiles you'll ever meet
has an enduring shyness behind stumbling lips.

❦

My smile is restless
until it touches your intoxicating lips.

❦

A Genuine Smile Is Your
Best Kind Of Yellow Teeth Relief

❦

The first time I smiled, it really wasn't a smile.
That is, my lips arched and pursed and suckled
and they all thought I smiled, but basically,
I had a feeling this is what one does
to feel safe after birth.

❦ ❦

Lips narrow and transfixed with a glaring smile
as if the blazing sun itself was trying
to peer into your deepest hidden sin.

Everything Goes With A Smile

He was depressed, his sad lips
unresistingly sinking into a torpid smile.

Her magnificent capacity for beautiful love making left
his lips physically burned out and empty but smile full.

She desires to give you the beauty of her smile,
the poetry of her delicious lips.

Lips were painted with bright red blood, all fear set aside,
with a savage smile willing to break stone into dust.

Her lips, once married to the
pure wisdom and goodness of God, now stared blank
with a meaningless smile of vanity and cross irritation.

✽

Good Karma Comes To Those That
Make Frequent Offerings Of A Smile.

✤

He marched a dark imperious smile
breathing large and wide while she knelt
slightly bowed with stiff curving lips.

Reflections on a Smile

Their mismatched lips coupled in
an erotic pool of warm spit, tongues playful
with slathering crystal clear smiles,
simple pure wondrousness.

Your lips become saturated with extraordinary smiles
upon graceful boundless compassion.

Beyond the radiant paleness of her lips a bright darkness
was filled with the holy light of her smile.

Survivors claim to have seen the great white light of
death and felt the inviting warmth of God on their lips
but skeptics explain it as an intoxicating neural
reflection of their own bright smile into the retina.

In a war of lips, smile is the first casualty.

Frost crunched lips stung with confession and
begged mercy the instant her laser penetrating eyes
rose above her disappointed but forgiving smile.

❋

Your Natural Born Smile Becomes
A Canvas Of Mother Nature's Artwork.

❋

A smile has certain gifts that if lips use appropriately,
will clear you a path calm and deep with miracles.

❋ ❋

If your lips flatly can't smile, you ought to
pee empty your swollen leather bladder brain
and sing gibberish until the struggles of life
are expelled from your heart and lungs.

❋ ❋ ❋

Oh that smile in heaven would brave pity
and grant mercy to the suffering lips in hell.

❋ ❋ ❋ ❋

Impoverished lips may be overwhelmed with shyness
but a helping smile can encourage magnificent
enthusiasm for real expressive talent in heart.

Reflections on a Smile

※ ※ ※

Looking across your swatch of sky
you might occasionally think your lips in love
painted a rainbow smile far and wide.

※ ※

To get a glimpse of holiness
steal a kiss from contagious sacred loving lips.

※

Extraordinary that a smile has no teeth!
There's never been a pair of lips that couldn't lure you
with it's smile and threaten to bite out your heart.

✼

To Smile Is Life And If Your Lips Live In Truth,
You Will Prosper Beyond Imagination.

※

No one is born without a smile
and no matter how many lips
are brought into this world crying, there's a
twinkling sweet spirit ready to surprise and awe.

※ ※

Her lips, hot as a naked candle,
burned a vivid graveyard smile
into his tombstone cool thoughts.

A Canvas Of Mother Nature's Artwork

Fat sensual lips hungry
for more wildly savage vigorous love
tucked away a hurricane smile
brewed from a storm in paradise.

You can't put your finger on a smile. There's a
certain careless pregnancy to it that lips usher to life.

His palsied smile did scream and shriek
with such a force that nearly
split his lips half-slung over nose.

Your lips warned me the high percentage
of butter love in their smile, but you should know
I'm into enriched high fat smiles.

※

Legend has a split army led by a lord with a man's rigid
crusty upper lip and woman's plump arched lower lip
bonded into a dragons boiling smile of unleashed power.

※

A Smile Has A Loveliness Which Can't Be Applied
Like Expensive Makeup On Beige Lips.

Reflections on a Smile

His square bony jaw set in a saintly face
that characterized stone pillars of faith
in a holy cathedral rocking you to salvation
as your blessed sleeping smile found solitude in
the simple quiet hallow sanctuary of God's love.

His fleshless skull boned smile stared at her suffering
wasted vile dirty twisting lips racked with dying sobs.

Lips have a need for time and season anticipating
hour by hour, but a smile just waits and waits for the
right moment lost somewhere in the protoplasm of life.

His lips felt short changed by her moneyed smile.

If there's even a little truth existing in that smile,
then those lips which God directly painted,
no matter how crude or false they appear,
have the essential components to bless mankind.

A smile strengthens lips
against the burdens they bear.

A Canvas Of Mother Nature's Artwork

Grieving lips carry a tremendous weight to exhaustion and might collapse into a death star if not for the saving gravitational pull of a compassionate smile.

Lips Have A Strength Of Will Able To Heal Or Harm.

A bottle of ruby throated wine accompanied by an earthen drinking vessel gladdened eyes and tongue of the rogue warrior whose devil lips smiled without exception on every brave belly that sheathed his sword.

Lips are never empty of smiles.
Some have perfect starbursts with hidden messages longing to be discovered and adopted.

Naked lips star struck under a kaleidoscope of hummingbirds flitting in the air between romancing smiles.

There's a cure waiting if someone smiles at you and you can't feel it. Your cold-heartedness needs an infusion of melting nuclear fission.

Reflections on a Smile

Spiritual insanity is the religious diagnosis
for a congregation of proselytizing lips sobbing with
praiseful smiles climbing on top of one another.

His wanting hypnotic smile breathed a deep kiss
into her attractive full lips that seized them both,
forever lost in a riptide of love in paradise.

Some people pass a collection plate around
to indulgent lips before they dispense a smile.

A Smile Isn't A Pill You Can Swallow With
A Glass Of Congeniality Hefted To Your Lips.

There's an innocent flirtation about some smiles,
as though a sudden cool thought or frill feeling
in a lover's lips might cause it to vanish.

Lips saw life as the original smile—
prayer and miracle unnecessary,
bad things whitewashed pure,
all invited to its magnificence.

A Canvas Of Mother Nature's Artwork

❋ ❋ ❋

His walking dead cocaine doped lips
managed to trickle out a final nut-hard smile.

❋ ❋ ❋ ❋

My lips always liked his smile
because it was the beginning
of a quiet evening in his arms.

❋ ❋ ❋

The blackest of his smile taints her pure lips
with wounded heart teardrops bleeding
perfect poison bishop's purple wine.

❋ ❋

Her pure lips bled wounded heart teardrops
after the blackest of his smile cussed a song
filled with perfect poison bishop's purple wine.

❋

She had a smile that could have
jumped off the Mona Lisa; sweet lips, pink cheeks,
adorable nose, Sistine Chapel architecture.

❋

A Smile Gets You To Places
Your Lips Could Never Reach.

Reflections on a Smile

The good manner of his lips is glued to a
beautiful body, but it is the space and depth of a smile
that intertwines the surroundings its creation.

I hovered near her lips
and felt my control slipping away
into animal desire
unable to think beyond a lustful smile.

Save your possessed heart,
part vestment lips from the altar of religiosity,
bathe and anoint your lovely lost spirit
with sanctified oil of myrrh,
ignite your smile with the flames
of a wasting silver candlestick,
all doubt boiled out of a stirred cauldron of pagan ritual.

Yes, yes! I have perfected my Venus de Mona Lisa smile
beyond the boundaries of my lips, even nature itself.

After death, everything that was behind the lips
can be willed to an eternity of inherited smiles.

A Canvas Of Mother Nature's Artwork

The phantom lips of that saintly girl's
daydreams hovered beyond shadows of reality.
Hi-ho, her smile resisted emergence from the
lost depths of sublime semiconscious hyper-sex.

His lashing pit bull smile left tremors in the earth
and flashed lightning across a trembling sky; the only
living memory of 10,000 lips kissing his sword of death.

✻

Lips Are Science By Illusion.
Smiles Are Magic In Reality.

Grit your teeth straight through your lower lip.
Drill cores of gnarled, bug infested emotions
out of your dead hearted smile.

Lips may be indecisive, but a smile lacks no courage
to cross the threshold of love.

Most smiles are good and sweet,
but there are some lips that jam-ruin it for everybody.

Reflections on a Smile

Lips and smile communicate
and influence each other with unutterable feelings.

For half a heart beat her lips expressed innocence hurt,
and then she thrust her head up away from my
insane groaning, tearing out a round and full smile.

A heart full of nestling love chickadees
spills abundant harmonies of tweets over smiling lips.

Her smile had the presence of a deity—
you could feel its wet sweetness around you
as defined as your lips kissing a ripe peeled peach.

Lips Can Be Private, Sometimes Intimate,
But A Smile Can Transfigure Your Spirit.

An old monk laughing hearty
with wine drunk belly shaking,
returns by stumble into his snore-house establishment,
lips flapping, smile jousting into
a vow of silence rich with passion.

A Canvas Of Mother Nature's Artwork

No man could resist her lips.
No man could endure her smile.

So sad for a smile to be condemned forever
to live detached from its lover's lips.

A shy smile foolishly imagines itself satisfied
in the safety of lips neither attractive nor repulsive,
but secretly hopes to bloom garlands of
seductive flowers with heart shaped petals
pressed between lovers locked in a kiss.

Surrender your smitten smile
to my sparkling flame of love and know the
rapture of naked lips trembling in their skin.

Her jasmine lips burnt through sultry hazy
dreams wrapped in the scent of a smile
left on his pillow by a former lover.

Lewd lips, if given half a chance, will suck salacious
every sweet drop of your innocent fragrant smile.

Biography

Dr. Lester Sawicki is an independent general dentist, practicing for more than 33 years. During the first 10 years of his career he directed a very successful practice in the Chicago area and since that time, has sustained recognition in Illinois, Pennsylvania, Texas, Nevada, New Jersey, Alabama, and Puerto Rico. Dr. Sawicki has contributed his knowledge and expertise to nearly 100 dental practices throughout the United States. In 1983, he began studying nutrition and alternative health, and since 2004 has been devoted to intensive research into the relationship between whole body detoxification and longevity. Dr. Sawicki's personal interests include martial arts and meditation. For 20 years he has been a practicing student of Tai Chi, having met many Tai Chi and Chi Kung Masters both in the United States and China. His home is in Austin, Texas.

www.ingramcontent.com/pod-product-compliance
Lightning Source LLC
Chambersburg PA
CBHW031406040426
42444CB00005B/436